Elizabeth —
You can keep this —
I thot you'd enjoy!
P—

I LOVE OLD THINGS

I LOVE OLD THINGS

HAROLD DARLING

BLUE LANTERN BOOKS
1998

ISBN 1-883211-09-3

BLUE LANTERN BOOKS
PO BOX 4399
SEATTLE, WASHINGTON 98104-0399

MOST PEOPLE LOVE NEWNESS. They glory in things new-made, primally clean, unmarked by use. They like chinaware gleaming in its fresh glaze, clocks that never need winding, books fresh from the press, the songs of the day, houses blank of other lives, the smell of a new car, chairs without troubled joints. They want new things around them because these make them feel fresh and clean, ready to step into life as one steps from a cool shower into a new day.

I understand these feelings, sometimes even share them, but mostly I LOVE OLD THINGS.

I LOVE OLD CITIES, those whose streets whisper the secrets of centuries, ones in which the buildings lean against one another like family dogs asleep.

I LOVE OLD HOUSES, those with crooked windows, rooms of all sizes, tall ceilings, soundless walls, basements, attics, shady yards, and tipsy chimneys.

5

I LOVE HOUSES WITH PORCHES that can be lived on, where the sound of a glider or the creak of a rocker is clear against the stillness, where fireflies float, and a pitcher of iced tea slowly mists.

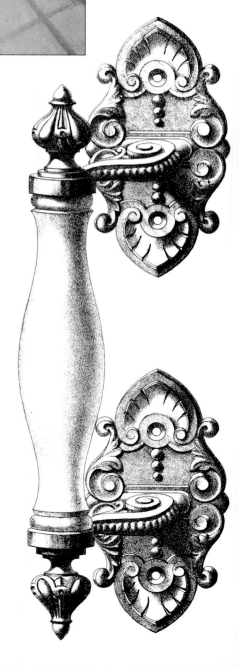

7

I LOVE OLD ROOMS, those with time-polished floors, deep fireplaces, many-paned windows – rooms filled with things and memories.

9

I WANT IN MY ROOMS FIRE that has been tamed. I want candle light, yellow and gentle, moving as the air moves, soft as a flower, making everything lovely. I want fire in a fireplace, groaning and spitting like a living being, making a room a place where one is never alone, inviting us to dream.

I LOVE OLD GARDENS,
ever changing, yet
recalling something of
their maker's plan,
places where one leaves
time for a paradise of
odors, colors, and
forms.

13

I LOVE OLD TREES, storm beaten whisperers, offering us in summer a world of shade, and in winter their bare beauty.

I LOVE OLD SHOPS, ones with crowded windows and overflowing shelves, places where the endless quest can be pursued, the unknown discovered, and rewards achieved.

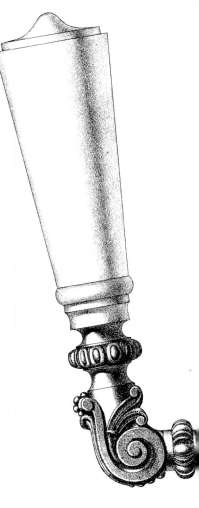

I LOVE OLD THINGS, ones that were made to last, and have lasted. I love them because they bring me closer to the past from which I grew, and to those who made and used them. I love them because I admire ingenuity, skill, and design, and because I feel that it is right to cherish that which has been cherished by those who came before me.

I LOVE OLD TOYS, ones that were made out of materials from our earth, that were intended to survive many children, many years. Such toys as these were created for the eternal child, rather than to satisfy fad or fashion. They make me want to touch and play with them.

Ball.

Doll.

Yacht.

Marbles.

Engine.

Paint-box and Brushes.

Toy Doggie.

HONOR C·APPLETON

21

BEST OF ALL OLD THINGS ARE OLD BOOKS, fragrant, subtle in their faded jackets, a limitless universe of knowledge and passion, waiting patiently for a reader to open them and enter.

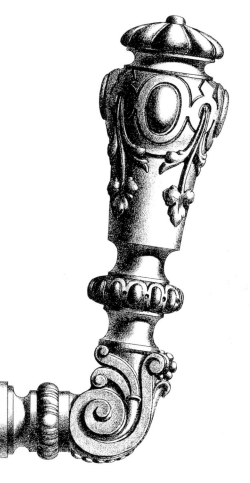

23

I LOVE THE OLD SONGS, the ones that people sang together through all the dramas of their lives, the songs that were passed like heirlooms from one generation to another, and are still remembered.

I LOVE THE OLD TALES, ones shaped over generations and proven good through the testing on listeners of all ages and kinds. Such tales as these never grow old.

I LOVE THE OLD WAY OF DOING THINGS, customs that sustain us by their constancy, and connect us with all those men and women who have gone before.

I LOVE THE OLD HOLIDAYS,
the ones which in my child-
hood were the high points
of the year. My parents

and their parents before them looked
forward to these days as avidly as I. The
celebration, the decoration, the family
meal – these are habits of the best kind.

I LOVE OLD RUINS for their melancholy splendor. They show me the persistence of beauty in the face of time.

PICTURE CREDITS

THIS BOOK IS TYPESET IN NEW BASKERVILLE.
BOOK & COVER DESIGN BY SACHEVERELL DARLING AT BLUE LANTERN STUDIO.

PRINTED IN HONG KONG THROUGH P. CHAN & EDWARD, INC